THE GENETIC CODE

R.B. ROMANIUK

About the Author

Mr. Roman B. Romaniuk earned his Bachelor of Science degree from the University of Toronto with majors in Biology and Chemistry. He subsequently worked for 5 years as a Molecular Biology Laboratory Technician at the world-renowned Basel Institute for Immunology which was located in Basel, Switzerland where he specialized in DNA splicing and gene cloning techniques. It was during this time of practical lab work that Mr. Romaniuk developed an in-depth understanding of the Genetic Code.

E-conversion of genetic code chart by Sweet 'N Spicy Designs, Tucson, Arizona.

Adobe InDesign Graphics done by KURZ DESIGN, Toronto, Canada.

THE GENETIC CODE

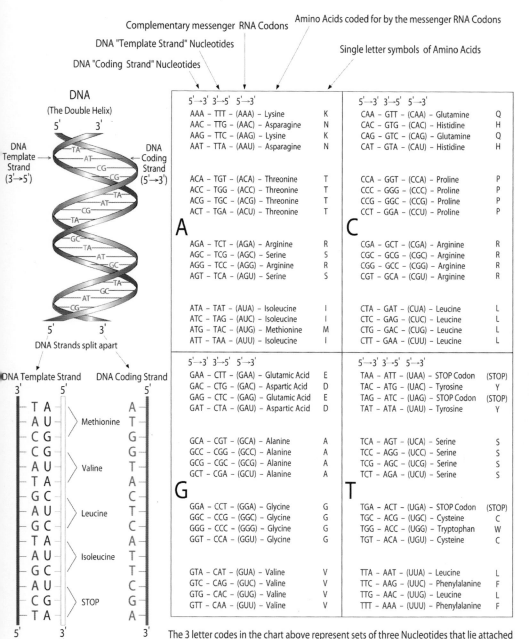

Complementary messenger RNA Codons

Amino Acids coded for by the messenger RNA Codons

DNA "Template Strand" Nucleotides

Single letter symbols of Amino Acids

DNA "Coding Strand" Nucleotides

DNA
(The Double Helix)

5'   3'

DNA Template Strand (3'→5')   DNA Coding Strand (5'→3')

5'   3'

DNA Strands split apart

DNA Template Strand   DNA Coding Strand

3'   5'   5'

T A	Methionine	A
A U		T
C G		G
C G		G
A U	Valine	T
T A		A
G C		C
A U	Leucine	T
G C		C
T A		A
A U	Isoleucine	T
G C		T
A U		C
C G	STOP	G
T A		A

5'   3'   3'

messenger RNA Strand

(With the help of an enzyme this mRNA molecule is formed as a kind of "coded-imprint" of the DNA Template Strand which is the "Printing-Plate" of the Genetic Code. This mRNA Strand then goes into the Protein-making factory of the cell to code for the one-by-one linking together of Amino Acids to form a Protein chain.)

Codon Table

5'→3' 3'→5' 5'→3'

A

AAA – TTT – (AAA) – Lysine	K
AAC – TTG – (AAC) – Asparagine	N
AAG – TTC – (AAG) – Lysine	K
AAT – TTA – (AAU) – Asparagine	N
ACA – TGT – (ACA) – Threonine	T
ACC – TGG – (ACC) – Threonine	T
ACG – TGC – (ACG) – Threonine	T
ACT – TGA – (ACU) – Threonine	T
AGA – TCT – (AGA) – Arginine	R
AGC – TCG – (AGC) – Serine	S
AGG – TCC – (AGG) – Arginine	R
AGT – TCA – (AGU) – Serine	S
ATA – TAT – (AUA) – Isoleucine	I
ATC – TAG – (AUC) – Isoleucine	I
ATG – TAC – (AUG) – Methionine	M
ATT – TAA – (AUU) – Isoleucine	I

C

CAA – GTT – (CAA) – Glutamine	Q
CAC – GTG – (CAC) – Histidine	H
CAG – GTC – (CAG) – Glutamine	Q
CAT – GTA – (CAU) – Histidine	H
CCA – GGT – (CCA) – Proline	P
CCC – GGG – (CCC) – Proline	P
CCG – GGC – (CCG) – Proline	P
CCT – GGA – (CCU) – Proline	P
CGA – GCT – (CGA) – Arginine	R
CGC – GCG – (CGC) – Arginine	R
CGG – GCC – (CGG) – Arginine	R
CGT – GCA – (CGU) – Arginine	R
CTA – GAT – (CUA) – Leucine	L
CTC – GAG – (CUC) – Leucine	L
CTG – GAC – (CUG) – Leucine	L
CTT – GAA – (CUU) – Leucine	L

5'→3' 3'→5' 5'→3'

G

GAA – CTT – (GAA) – Glutamic Acid	E
GAC – CTG – (GAC) – Aspartic Acid	D
GAG – CTC – (GAG) – Glutamic Acid	E
GAT – CTA – (GAU) – Aspartic Acid	D
GCA – CGT – (GCA) – Alanine	A
GCC – CGG – (GCC) – Alanine	A
GCG – CGC – (GCG) – Alanine	A
GCT – CGA – (GCU) – Alanine	A
GGA – CCT – (GGA) – Glycine	G
GGC – CCG – (GGC) – Glycine	G
GGG – CCC – (GGG) – Glycine	G
GGT – CCA – (GGU) – Glycine	G
GTA – CAT – (GUA) – Valine	V
GTC – CAG – (GUC) – Valine	V
GTG – CAC – (GUG) – Valine	V
GTT – CAA – (GUU) – Valine	V

T

TAA – ATT – (UAA) – STOP Codon	(STOP)
TAC – ATG – (UAC) – Tyrosine	Y
TAG – ATC – (UAG) – STOP Codon	(STOP)
TAT – ATA – (UAU) – Tyrosine	Y
TCA – AGT – (UCA) – Serine	S
TCC – AGG – (UCC) – Serine	S
TCG – AGC – (UCG) – Serine	S
TCT – AGA – (UCU) – Serine	S
TGA – ACT – (UGA) – STOP Codon	(STOP)
TGC – ACG – (UGC) – Cysteine	C
TGG – ACC – (UGG) – Tryptophan	W
TGT – ACA – (UGU) – Cysteine	C
TTA – AAT – (UUA) – Leucine	L
TTC – AAG – (UUC) – Phenylalanine	F
TTG – AAC – (UUG) – Leucine	L
TTT – AAA – (UUU) – Phenylalanine	F

The 3 letter codes in the chart above represent sets of three Nucleotides that lie attached to one another in a row along a single strand of DNA and/or messenger RNA. Nucleotides are organic compounds that contain the atoms Phosphorus, Oxygen, Nitrogen, Carbon and Hydrogen (PONCH) and serve as the building blocks of the Nucleic Acids. The 4 types of Nucleotides that are components of DNA contain the following Nitrogenous Bases: Adenine (A), Cytosine (C), Guanine (G) and Thymine (T). The 4 types of Nucleotides that are components of RNA contain the following Nitrogenous Bases: Adenine (A), Cytosine (C), Guanine (G) and Uracil (U). The single letter symbols for the amino acids in the far right column of each box are used to denote amino acid sequences of Proteins in current scientific journals and computer data bases found on the Internet.

CONTENTS

GENETIC CODE CHART EXPLANATION
KEY WORDS

K*ey Words*: DNA, Deoxyribonucleic Acid, Deoxyribose sugar, RNA, Ribonucleic Acid, Ribose sugar, messenger RNA, Nitrogenous base, Adenine, Cytosine, Guanine, Thymine, Uracil, Phosphate, Nucleotide, Nucleotide triplet (N-triplet), Amino Acids, Polarity, Anti-parallel, Phosphodiester linkage.

Chart Organization

This uniquely organized Genetic Code Chart clearly illustrates the following in horizontal "left-to-right" lines: the Nucleotide triplets (i.e. N-triplets) of the DNA Coding Strand, the N-triplets of the complementary DNA Template Strand, the N-triplets of the complementary messenger RNA

Codons and the Amino Acids that the mRNA Codons code for.

The chart is divided up into 4 main boxes, with each box designated with a large bold letter A, C, G or T on the left side of each box. To easily zero-in on any DNA Coding Strand N-triplet that starts with either A, C, G or T, the user simply has to know the first letter of the N-triplet of the DNA Coding Strand and look at the box with that large letter on its left side.

Example: If the DNA Coding Strand N-triplet happens to be (ATC), that N-triplet starts with the letter "A". One simply looks at the box with the large letter "A" on its left side and looks down the first column in that box to easily pinpoint the Nucleotide triplet in question that starts with the letter "A" (in our example ATC). By doing so, one can read off from left to right, the DNA Coding Strand N-triplet (ATC), the complementary DNA Template Strand N-triplet (TAG), the complementary messenger RNA Codon (AUC) and the corresponding Amino Acid that is coded for by that specific mRNA Codon (in this case, Isoleucine). To the extreme right side of each box is a column with the single letter biochemical designation for the amino acid in question.

GENETIC CODE CHART EXPLANATION

DNA (DEOXYRIBONUCLEIC ACID)

DNA is made up of 2 single strands that wind around each other to result in the shape of a Double Helix. Each single strand of DNA is made up of covalently linked molecules called Nucleotides that contain Nitrogenous Bases. The 4 Nitrogenous Bases found in DNA are: Adenine (A), Cytosine (C), Guanine (G) and Thymine (T). The 4 letters of the DNA Genetic Code are: A, C, G and T. These letters stand for the Nitrogenous Bases: Adenine, Cytosine, Guanine and Thymine. The nitrogenous bases are components of longer molecules that are called Nucleotides which are the actual building blocks of DNA strands. The DNA double helix has a sugar-phosphate backbone whereby the sugar subunits are covalently linked to phosphate groups by way of phosphodiester linkages.

Molecular Structure of DNA Nucleotides

DNA Nucleotides are made up of: a Nitrogenous Base (either one of A, C, G or T) that is covalently linked to a deoxyribose sugar molecule, which in turn is covalently linked to a phosphate molecule.

Example: A **Nucleotide** which contains the Nitrogenous Base *Adenine* (A):

Nitrogenous Base (A) + Deoxyribose sugar + Phosphate molecule =

Nucleotide containing Adenine. (*A building block of a DNA strand*).

In the above example, you can substitute the letter (A) with either (C, G, or T) in making a nucleotide that goes into the formation of a DNA molecule.

Important note: in DNA, the sugar component **must** be **D**eoxyribose. That is why there is the letter "**D**" in DNA.

GENETIC CODE CHART EXPLANATION

RNA (RIBONUCLEIC ACID)

RNA is also made up of molecules called Nucleotides that contain 4 Nitrogenous Bases. The 4 Nitrogenous Bases found in RNA are: Adenine (A), Cytosine (C), Guanine (G) and Uracil (U). One key difference between DNA and RNA is that DNA can contain the Nitrogenous bases A, C, G and T whereas RNA can contain the Nitrogenous bases A, C, G, and U.

To Summarize: RNA can contain the 4 Nitrogenous Bases (A,C,G,U), whereas DNA can contain the 4 Nitrogenous Bases (A,C,G,T). There is no Thymine (T) in RNA and there is no Uracil (U) in DNA.

Molecular Structure of RNA Nucleotides

RNA Nucleotides are made up of: A Nitrogenous Base (either one of A, C, G or U) that is covalently linked to a ribose sugar molecule, which in turn is covalently linked to a phosphate molecule.

Example: An RNA Nucleotide which contains the Nitrogenous Base Uracil (U):

Nitrogenous Base (U) + Ribose sugar + Phosphate molecule =

RNA Nucleotide containing Uracil. (*A building block of an RNA strand*).

In the above example, you can substitute the letter (U) with either (A, C or G) in making a nucleotide that goes into the making of an RNA molecule.

Important Note in RNA, the sugar component **must** be **R**ibose. That is why there is the letter **"R"** in RNA.

There are different types of RNA molecules, but each type is made up of combinations of the same 4 Nitrogenous bases (i.e. Adenine, Cytosine, Guanine and Uracil).

Different types of RNA molecules are: messenger RNA, transfer RNA and ribosomal RNA.

The one type of RNA that is in this Genetic Code Chart is: ***messenger RNA***.

GENETIC CODE CHART EXPLANATION
COMPLEMENTARY BASE PAIRING RULE

n the DNA double helix, (A) always pairs with (T) and (G) always pairs with (C). The two single chains of nucleotides in DNA are held together in a double helix structure by Hydrogen bonds between the Nitrogenous bases.

So, **A** in one strand of DNA always bonds with **T** in the other strand via 2 hydrogen bonds,

and **G** in one strand of DNA always bonds with **C** in the other strand via 3 hydrogen bonds.

Complementary Base Pairing Rule between DNA and messenger RNA.

A single strand of DNA binds with a single strand of messenger RNA via hydrogen bonds as well.

An A in DNA always pairs with a U in messenger RNA via 2 hydrogen bonds,

and T in DNA always pairs with an A in messenger RNA via 2 hydrogen bonds,

and G in DNA always pairs with a C in messenger RNA via 3 hydrogen bonds,

and C in DNA always pairs with a G in messenger RNA via 3 hydrogen bonds.

On the Genetic Code Chart we can look at an example of this Complementary Base Pairing Rule as you read each horizontal line from left to right.

Example: On the top horizontal line in the "A" box, from left to right, you see the following headings pointing to the 3 vertical columns:

DNA "Coding Strand" 3-Letter Code: AAA

DNA "Template Strand" 3-Letter Code: TTT

Complementary messenger RNA Codon: (AAA)

Amino Acid coded for by the 3-Letter Codon: Lysine

GENETIC CODE CHART EXPLANATION
POLARITY AND ANTI-PARALLEL ORIENTATION OF THE 2 DNA STRANDS OF A DOUBLE HELIX.

As you can see in the left-most margin of the Genetic Code Chart, there is the Double Helix structure of a DNA molecule. One strand is red in colour and the other strand is blue. The red-coloured strand is labeled at the top of it as 5′ and if you follow the red swirl down to the bottom, it is labeled as 3′. The little superscript tick at the top right side of the numbers 5 and 3 represent the word "prime". So, the opposite ends of any single DNA strand are referred to as 5 prime and 3 prime ends (i.e. 5′ and 3′ ends).

Now if you look at the top of the blue strand, it is labeled as 3′ and if you follow it all the way down, its bottom end is labeled as 5'. In any DNA double helix, when the 2 separate strands come together, one of them is always linearly aligned in the 5' to 3' direction while the other strand is in the 3' to 5' direction.

Any single strand of DNA is said to have "Polarity" in that one end of the chain is always a 5' end and the opposite end is always a 3' end. This is called the "Polarity" of a DNA strand. RNA molecules also exhibit this same type of polarity.

The 5' end is called that because the phosphate group at the end is covalently bonded to the 5' carbon atom of the deoxyribose sugar molecule.

The 3' end is called that because an hydroxyl group (OH) is attached to the 3' carbon atom of the deoxyribose sugar molecule.

The "Anti-parallel" orientation of DNA single strands in a double helix refers to the fact that when the 2 strands come together, they are oriented in opposite directions with regard to their 5' and 3' polarity.

Example: In the coloured illustration of the vertical DNA molecule in the left margin on the chart, one

strand from top to bottom is in the 5′ to 3′ orientation whereas the opposite strand is in the 3′ to 5′
orientation. This is what is referred to as the "Anti-
parallel orientation" of the 2 DNA strands.

GENETIC CODE CHART EXPLANATION

DEFINITION OF DNA "CODING STRAND" VS DNA "TEMPLATE STRAND"

The DNA molecule is composed of 2 separate polynucleotide strands that are held together by Hydrogen Bonds between the Nitrogenous Bases of the separate strands to form a double helix. The Nitrogenous Bases are situated on the inside of the double helix and face each other.

There are definitions for the 2 strands of DNA on the internet that can be confusing to the student of molecular biology. Please pay close attention to the following explanation.

The **DNA Template Strand** is the DNA strand that serves as the "printing plate" so to speak of the genetic code, and is read by the RNA Polymerase enzyme molecule during the process of Transcription for the formation of a messenger RNA strand.

The DNA Template Strand is read by RNA polymerase in the 3' to 5' direction of the DNA Template Strand. The DNA Template Strand Nucleotides are red as triplets and are transcribed into a Complimentary sequence of messenger RNA that is formed in the 5' to 3' direction of the growing messenger RNA strand.

For example: on the first horizontal line in the A box of the Genetic Code chart, the DNA Coding Strand triplet reads like this: 5' to 3' AAA. The **DNA Template Strand** triplet reads like this: 3' to 5' TTT. So the corresponding messenger RNA triplet that is transcribed is: 5' to 3' AAA. As you can see, the complementary base pairing rule is observed as is the anti-parallel rule.

The **DNA Coding Strand** is called that because its sequence of genetic code letters is the same as the **Codons** of the **messenger RNA** that will be translated into a chain of amino acids that make up proteins (and both sets of N-triplets are in the same 5' $\rightarrow$ 3' orientation. See below). The one exception to the sameness of the code is that whenever there is a "T" in the DNA Coding Strand, there is a "U" in the messenger RNA strand.

Example:

$$5' \to 3' \ 5' \to 3'$$

DNA Coding Strand ACC→ mRNA Codon (ACC) Same letters for both.

$$5' \to 3' \ 5' \to 3'$$

BUT DNA Coding Strand ACT→ mRNA Codon (ACU) 3rd base is different.

––––––––––––

Hopefully, you have found this booklet of basic facts about DNA and the Genetic Code helpful in your Biology course study program. The Chart itself was designed to provide quick and easy genetic code information regarding the Codons of the DNA Coding Strand, the DNA Template Strand, the messenger RNA strand as well as the Amino Acids that are coded for. All of this information can be seen at a glance in one horizontal line for all 64 Codons of the Genetic Code.

NOTES

Printed in Great Britain
by Amazon